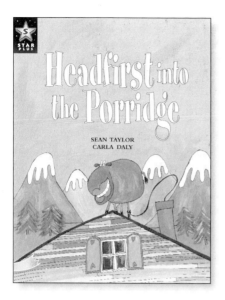

The front cover

What type of story is this going to be? How do you know? (*humorous – title, illustration*)

Have we read any other stories by this author? (*The Woodcutter and the Bear*)

The back cover

Let's read the blurb together.

How do you think Benni will get on with Anna's chores?

The title page

What do you think is cooking in the pot?

What clues does this give us about the story?

Lesson 1 (Chapter 1)

READ

Read pages 2 to 4

Purpose: To find out what Anna's chores are.

PAUSE

Pause at page 4

Where is the story set? Which words tell you? (*a small farm in the hills*)

Why did Anna and Benni decide to swap jobs?

In what order should Benni do the chores?

Chapter 1

Anna and Benni had a small farm in the hills. They had one brown cow, some hens, a sheep, a goat, and a big field of hay. They lived in a little wooden house in the shelter of a grassy mound.

One morning, Benni sat down on his old rocking chair and sighed.

"Why are you huffing and puffing?" Anna asked.

"I'm tired," said Benni, "and I've got to cut the hay."

"You're just lazy!" said Anna.

Benni frowned. "You'd complain too, if you had to do what I do!" he said.

"Are you sure?" asked Anna.

"Oh, yes. As sure as a man can be!" said Benni. "I do more work in one day than you do in three."

"Well, if that's what you think," said Anna, "then why don't I cut the hay? You can stay here and do the things that I usually do."

"All right," said Benni.

"You can start by pouring the tea," said Anna.

"What do I have to do then?" asked Anna.

"Cut all the hay in the field," said Benni.

"And I suppose all I have to do is rock the baby and make the bed?"

"That's right," said Anna. "And feed the sheep, and milk the goat, and clean out the chicken coop, and sweep the floor, and beat the rug, and chop the wood, and wash the sheets, and make the fire, and cook the porridge, and take the brown cow down to the grassy field."

READ

Read pages 6 to 9

Purpose: To find out what Benni did next.

PAUSE

Pause at page 9

Did Benni start the chores in the right order?

What has he still got left to do?

Is Benni right in thinking the chores won't take long?

What do you think has happened while Benni was down in the cellar? What clues did you use to help you? (*illustration – sheep coming through open door*)

Anna set off for the hayfield, and Benni sat down with a smile. "Well, this will be a fine day," he said. "Those chores won't take long."

He stretched his legs and looked around the room. "I might just drink another quick cup of tea," he thought. He drank his tea and sighed happily.

"Those chores won't take long. They won't take long at all," he said to himself. "Maybe I'll have a small cheese sandwich."

He started his sandwich and fell asleep by the warm fire.

An hour later he woke up. "Well," he yawned. "I'd better get those chores done."

So, he made the bed, and rocked the baby, and put the food for the sheep in a sack by the door.

Then he found the broom and swept the floor.

He sharpened the axe, chopped the wood, and tied up the goat.

He milked the goat, took the milk bucket indoors, and put the sheets in the washtub.

Then he took the rug outside and started to beat it.

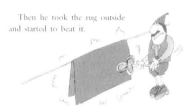

All this hard work was making him thirsty! "I'll just go and get a cup of apple cider," thought Benni.

Benni went down to the cellar. The apple cider was in a large barrel. Benni put his cup under the tap and turned it on when suddenly . . .

CRASH!

READ

Read pages 10 to 11

Purpose: To find confirm predictions.

PAUSE

Pause at page 11

What do you think the strange swooshing sound is?

Benni rushed back upstairs.

The sheep had come in through the open door and was standing in the kitchen. It had knocked the milk all over the floor.

Benni splashed through the milk and herded the sheep out of the door.

Benni was mopping up the mess when he heard a strange swooshing sound from downstairs.

"What could that be?" he thought. Benni hurried back down to the cellar and . . .

7

READ

Read pages 12 to 14

Purpose: To confirm predictions.

PAUSE

Pause at page 14

What has Benni still got to do?

Why is Benni having problems with Anna's chores?

How do you think Anna is getting on in the hayfield?

Please turn to page 16 for Revisit and Respond activities.

He saw that he had left the tap running. He was up to his ankles in apple cider. Just then, the baby started to scream, so he rushed upstairs again.

12

Benni rocked the baby and washed the sheets in the washtub. Then he scrubbed the floor and cleaned out the chicken coop.

Then he hung out the sheets, and at that second . . .

13

Benni ran inside and dropped into his old rocking chair. "I'm so tired!" he thought. "I'll just take a little nap."

But when he saw the time he was so surprised that he almost fell off his chair. Anna would be back any minute!

14

Lesson 2 (Chapter 2)

RECAP

Recap lesson 1

What chores did Benni have to do? Re-read page 4 to help you.

What has Benni done so far? What has he still got left to do?

READ

Read pages 15 to 17

Purpose: To find out whether Benni completes his chores before Anna comes back.

PAUSE

Pause at page 17

Has Benni completed all his chores?

Will Anna be pleased when she gets back?

Chapter 2

Benni had just five minutes to make the porridge and take the brown cow down to the grassy field.

"Anna won't be at all happy if these chores aren't done!" he said to himself.

So he found the oats, stoked the fire, and put the porridge in the pot. Then he stopped. How was he going to take the brown cow down to the grassy field, *and* stir the porridge at the same time?

He rubbed his chin and stared into the fire.

Suddenly, he remembered the grassy mound behind the house. The cow could graze there.

He rushed outside, tied a rope around the cow's leg, and took her up onto the grassy mound.

Then he dropped the rope down the chimney.

He ran back to the fireplace, and tied the other end of the rope around his ankle.

"Now the brown cow can't run off," he said to himself, "and the porridge will still be ready on time."

READ

Read pages 18 to 19

Purpose: To find out if Benni has any more problems.

PAUSE

Pause at page 19

What is going to happen next?

Will Anna be cross with Benni?

However, the brown cow had never eaten on the grassy mound before. She was used to the grassy field, which was long and flat. There she would walk and eat, walk and eat, and she never bothered to look where she was going.

So now she just kept on walking and kept on eating. Soon, she had plodded onto the roof of the house and was eating the grass that grew in the gutters.

Benni was so busy stirring the porridge that he didn't notice the rope disappearing up the chimney.

The brown cow kept walking across the roof, and when she came to the edge, she fell off!

The rope yanked Benni by the ankle and . . .

whoops!

Benni went flying up the chimney!

READ

Read pages 20 to the end

Purpose: To confirm predictions.

PAUSE

Pause at page 24

Why didn't Anna rescue Benni from the chimney first?

Why did Benni decide to cut the hay the next day?

Why wasn't Anna cross with him?

What could be another title for this story?

At that moment, Anna came back from the hayfield. She saw the sheets hanging in the rain and the brown cow hanging from the roof.

"Benni!" she yelled, bursting into the house. All she could see was a pot of porridge bubbling over the fire. She couldn't imagine where Benni was or why he had hung the brown cow from the roof.

"MOOOOOOOOOOOOOOO!!!" complained the brown cow.

Anna rushed out, cut the rope, and . . .

well, you can guess what happened next!

21

14

"MOO!" cried the cow, as she landed back on the ground.

"WHAAAAAAAAAAAAARGH!" screamed Benni as he fell down the chimney and headfirst into the porridge!

Anna laughed until she cried.

"Tomorrow I'm going to cut the hay!" said Benni, trying to scrape porridge out of his hair.

Anna looked at him, wiping the tears from her eyes. "Are you sure?" she asked.

"Oh, yes," said Benni. "As sure as a man can be!"

After Reading

Revisit and Respond

Lesson 1

T) Which parts of the story have the children found funny?

T) Remind the children of *The Woodcutter and the Bear* by the same author. Return to the list made after reading *The Woodcutter and the Bear* and compare the stories. What has the author done that is the same? What is different?

T) What will Anna find when she comes back?

Lesson 2

S) Ask the children to pick out the commas in the second sentence on page 2. Then ask one of the children to read the second sentence aloud, as if there were no commas. Why are commas used here?

S) Now look at the list of chores on page 4. Ask the children, in pairs, to write a list of the chores in the order Benni did them. Remind them to use commas to separate the items in the list.

T) Ask the children to think about other funny stories they have read (*The School Concert* and *A Mammoth Mistake*). What makes this story funny? Is the author's style similar to that in *The School Concert* or *A Mammoth Mistake?*